Random Thoughts

How Reading Helped Me Make Sense Of My Thinking

By

Avien & Virgil Abney

NoFame Mjollniir Publishing

Copyright 2017©. All rights reserved.

ISBN-13: 978-0-9996849-0-0

ATTENTION CORPORATIONS, UNIVERSITIES, COLLEGES, PROFESSIONAL ORGANIZATIONS PUBLIC and CHARTER SCHOOLS: Quantity discounts are available on bulk purchases of this book for educational purposes, or as premiums for increasing magazine subscriptions or renewals. Special books or book excerpts can also be created to fit specific needs. For more information, please contact NoFame Mjollniir Publishing utilizing the QR code on the rear panel of this book.

Although the author and publisher has made every effort to ensure the accuracy and completeness of information contained in this book, we assume no responsibility for errors, inaccuracies, omissions or any inconsistency herein. Any slights of people, places or organizations are unintentional.

Dedications

Doris, Billy, Amber, Alaya,
Myra, Katrina and Nathan.

For your unwavering support, unconditional love, patience and understanding. Your belief in our ability to effect positive change in the world has always kept our desire to achieve this goal intact despite the obstacles that had been placed before us. May this book serve as proof-positive of your convictions as well as a perpetual memorial of our gratitude.

"I hear and I forget. I see and I remember. I do and I understand."

- Confucius

A MESSAGE TO PARENTS

This book is designed to achieve two primary functions. The first function is to help you understand that the role you play in your child's academic growth is a critical one. Parents must have a general idea of the weaknesses in their child's academic abilities so that they can assist their child in overcoming them. How do you achieve this? Begin by reaching out to your child's teachers if you haven't already done so.

Knowing what your child is doing in class will give you an idea about what you need to do at home. Parents gain this knowledge by asking questions. Questions such as: "What do you see as my child's strengths?" "Is my child performing on grade level?" "In what areas is my child having the most problems?" are good ways to begin this process. Most important-ly, ask questions even if your child is performing well. Regardless of your child's grade status, you should always monitor your child's academic development to ensure the progress of their learning.

The second function of this book is to provide a practical way to empower parents to fulfill an active role as their child's educational advocate. Parents are encouraged to read the story __with__ their child and go over a challenge __with__ their child at the end of each week until their child has mastered each challenge. Research any words, parts of speech or concepts in this book that you do not fully understand. Not only will this maximize your child's potential for growth, it will maximize your potential for growth as well. Congratulations on your impending success.

COMPREHENSION CHECK SYSTEM

Comprehension Check Indicators have been placed throughout this book and are to be used to measure your child's level of comprehension in relation to the content imparted in this book. The scholar is to be awarded the point values for each question answered correctly. Examples are placed below. Once all the questions and challenges have been completed, the point value of each correctly answered question is to be added. The highest number of points that the scholar may achieve is 103. The value of the prize that you award your child should match the score result that your child achieves.

Comprehension Check Question

Comprehension Check Indicator

Comprehension Check Point Value

COM-CHECK: WHO IS THE MAIN CHARACTER OF THE STORY? = 5 PTS

Comprehension Check Instruction

Comprehension Check Point Value

= 1 PT

DRAW A LINE FROM
PUNCTUATION TO FUNCTION

OPERATION:

The content of this book was developed using the same sources and standards used by public and charter schools in the development of their curriculum. The charts below highlights those target areas we have deemed most important and wish for you to focus on while you assist your child with working through the story and challenges in this book. We recommend that you begin with the first 11 target areas as a mastery of these concepts will give your child the foundation needed to achieve maximum fluency in the remaining target areas.

☐	Reader is able to identify a **_noun_** and its function.
☐	Reader is able to identify a **_verb_** and its function.
☐	Reader is able to identify an **_adjective_** and its function.
☐	Reader is able to identify a **_conjunction_** and its function.
☐	Reader is able to identify a **_period_** and its function.
☐	Reader is able to identify a **_question mark_** and its function.
☐	Reader is able to identify an **_exclamation point_** and its function.
☐	Reader is able to identify **_quotation marks_** and their function.
☐	Reader is able to identify a **_semicolon_** and its function.
☐	Reader is able to identify a **_comma_** and its function.
☐	Reader is able to identify an **_apostrophe_** and its function.
☐	Reader is able to **_recall events in chronological order_**.
☐	Reader is able to **_connect events logically_**.

"MONITOR YOUR CHILD'S PROGRESS"

It is vital, to the positive development of your child's ability to comprehend messages through reading, that he/she has a strong knowledge of the basic parts of speech, punctuation and other concepts presented in this book. At the end of the story, you will find several guides that are designed to help your child achieve this goal. Parents are urged to study these guides _with_ their child. Once your child has mastered a skill indicated in one of the charts, make a check mark in the red box next to the skill that has been mastered. Continue doing this until all target areas have been mastered.

☐	Reader is able to to **_explain reasons behind events_**.
☐	Reader is able to **_use text evidence to support reasoning_**.
☐	Reader is able to **_distinguish own point of view from characters_**.
☐	Reader is able to **_compare points of view_**.
☐	Reader is able to **_identify the points of view of characters_**.
☐	Reader is able to **_draw logical conclusions from text_**.
☐	Reader is able to **_gather information_** from illustrations, maps, etc.
☐	Reader is able to **_use search tools_**. (I.e. Dictionary, Internet, etc.)
☐	Reader is able to **_ask and answer questions relevant to text_**.
☐	Reader is able to **_identify misspelled words_**.
☐	Reader is able to **_introduce a topic through writing_**.
☐	Reader is able to **_provide details through writing_**.
☐	Reader is able to **_provide a conclusion through writing_**.

STOP!

Scholar's Agreement

PARENT/SCHOLAR CHALLENGE CONTRACT

SCHOLAR'S PLEDGE

I _____, will read one book a week for a one month time period; beginning on date:_____, and ending on date:_____. I will do this **without being told to do so**. After reading each book, I will answer the questions in **Challenge # 3** for each book that I read during this time period. I understand that this particular challenge only counts as one full point once I complete it, but will count as a 20 point deduction from my overall score if I fail to do so. I will also complete the remaining **Challenges** and each **Com-Check Indicator** in the story section which is **19** in all.

PARENT'S PLEDGE

I _____, will be an active agent in the positive academic development of my child. In relation to the material contained in this book, I will guide my child through its' lessons; assisting my child when it is needed. In addition, I will assess my child in accordance with the point value system set forth in this book. When my child has successfully completed all of the **Challenges** and **Com-Check Indicator** questions contained in this book, I will award my child with a reasonably priced prize of my child's choosing.

Hello, my name is Avien and I have a question I would like to ask you:

"Do you like to read?"

AW MAN!

Well if not, let me share my story with you. During my younger years, before I had learned how to read, my family and teachers would often read to me. The time they took to read to me helped me learn a lot of new and interesting things. As time passed and I learned to read on my own, I realized something. I do not like to read.

Although I don't like to read, my family and teachers make me read often. This upsets me at times because I would rather be doing other things. I am glad they do make me read because I realized that, when I don't read, my mind becomes clouded with random thoughts.

A random thought is an idea that you do not fully understand because you do not have enough information to help give it context. Context is the additional information an idea needs to be better understood. Reading provides this information. Let's show you how.

One day, I was riding in the car with my dad. As we were passing a grocery store, a random thought popped into my mind. "Hmm...Grossceries," I thought. After a moment of thinking, I turned to my dad and said "Dad, why would someone want to open a grocery store?"

After stopping at a red light, my dad sat and reflected on my question for a while before he turned and looked at me. Then, with a puzzled look on his face, he said "What do you mean son?" I responded, saying "Why do people want to buy gross things?"

Amused by my question, my dad chuckled and stared at me for a moment. Then, after what seemed like an eternity, he said "The answer to your question is not a simple one. You will need to gather more information. Wait until we are home and I will help you find the answer." The traffic light turned green again and so we continued on our way.

Once we were home, my dad sat me down at his desk and turned on the computer. He placed his fingertips on the keyboard and began typing.

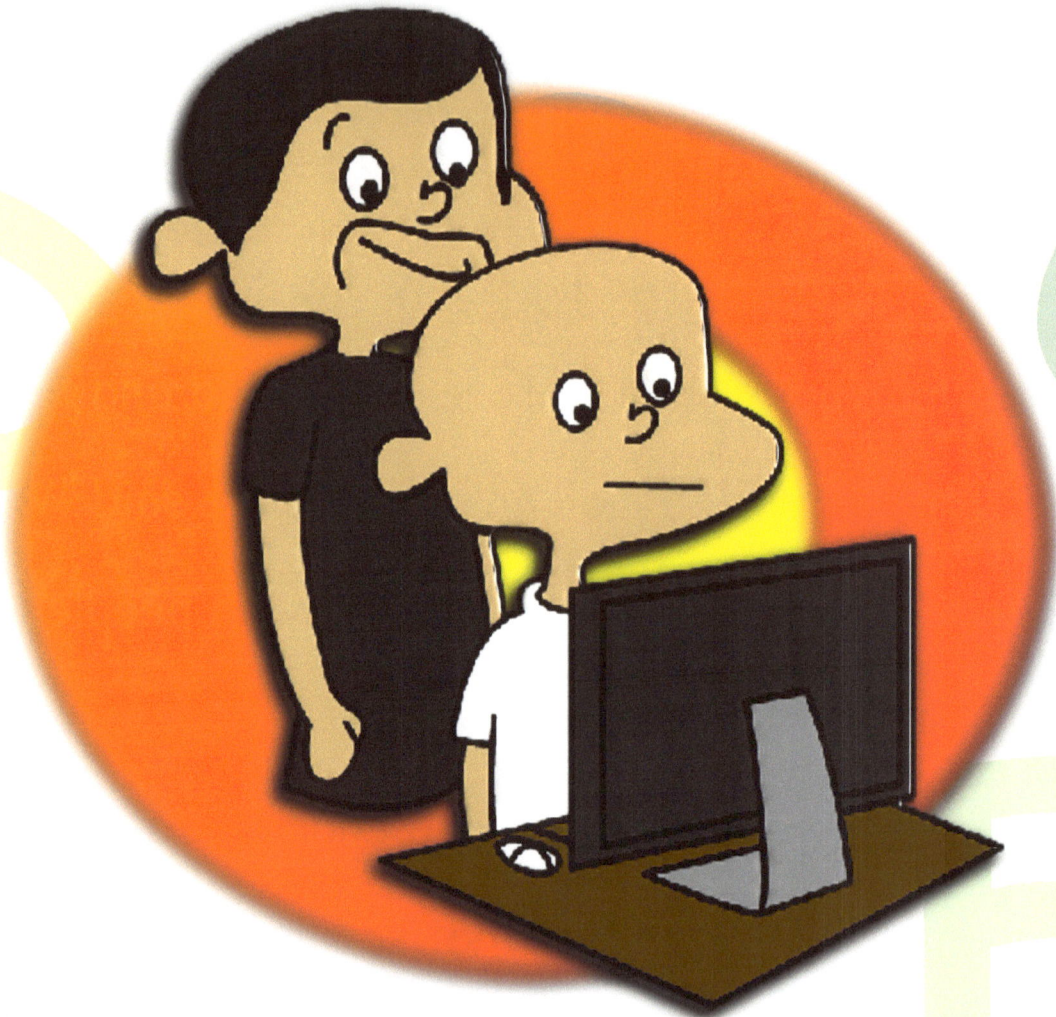

As he typed, he directed my attention to the screen and showed me how to find an online dictionary. Next, he helped me find the words: "Gross" and "Grocery." I then read their meanings.

Upon reading, I learned that "Grossceries" is not a word. What I had done was confuse the two words: "Gross" and "Grocery." Not only is each word spelled differently, they also have different meanings. I have turned the computer around so you can read their meanings too.

"GROSSCERIES"

GROSS
Strong feelings of dislike.

GROCERY
A store selling food and other needed things.

Another thing that I learned is that grocery stores do not sell gross things but there are some groceries that may be considered gross to some people and not gross to others, like onions.

My dad loves onions, I don't. Not only do I dislike their taste, I don't like their smell either.

PHEW!

KNOW SNOW

Reading also helped me make sense of the random thoughts I've had about winter which is my favorite time of the year.

COM-CHECK: WHAT IS WINTER USED TO DESCRIBE? = 5 PTS

For example, I learned some things about snow that I didn't know before. First, I learned that snowflakes are small bits of frozen water that fall from the sky.

Second, I learned that water reaches the sky as a vapor. When too much moisture collects in our atmosphere, the cold winter air freezes the vapor which forms into ice crystals that fall from the sky in a large variety of different shapes and sizes.

Snow is a form of precipitation. Do you know what precipitation is? Precipitation is any form of water that falls from the sky. Other forms of precipitation are rain, hail and sleet.

Third, I learned that snow has many effects. An "Effect" is the result of something. For example, snowy hills are one effect of snowfall. When large amounts of snow fall from the sky, snowy hills begin to form. Large snowy hills are my favorite, and the most fun, because I slide really fast when I ride my sled down them.

SWOOSH!

Some of the effects of snow are not fun and even dangerous. One of these effects is "Frostbite." Frostbite is damage that is caused to your skin when it is in contact with the cold snow for too long.

Snow is cold and if I am not dressed in the proper clothing, the cold snow can damage my skin. You should always dress in the proper clothing when out in the snow because not only does frost-bite damage your skin, it is also very painful.

OUCH!

Lastly, when snow covers the ground, the roads and sidewalks become really slippery. This condition makes it dangerous for people who walk on the sidewalks and drive on the roads. You can slip and fall when you are walking or hit something when you're driving.

WHOOPS!

My advice to people who walk or drive when the ground is covered with snow is "Be careful!"

COM-CHECK: WHAT IS ADVICE?   = 5 PTS

As you can see from what I have shared with you in earlier parts of my story, reading can help you make sense of many of the random thoughts that cloud your mind. By using your ability to carefully examine written words, you are able to grasp their meanings. As a result, you are able to uncover new ideas and gain the insight that you need to bring order to any confusion you may have about a person, place or thing.

While I still don't like to read, I recognize that just because I do not like to read does not mean that I should not read. Reading helps my mind grow, and provides me with the information that I need to achieve my goals. It transforms written information into knowledge. The most important thing that I think reading has taught me is that, in order to make sense of the random thoughts in my mind and the world around me, I must read.

Even my family has made sense of their random thoughts through reading and I am sure that reading will help you make sense of your random thoughts too. So, keep reading and be well!

GUIDE #1

BUILDING-BLOCKS OF READING

Parts of Speech

Noun	A *Person*, *Place* or *Thing*.
Verb	Tells you what a Person or Thing *is doing*.
Adjective	*Describes* a Person, Place or Thing.

Sentence Structure

Sentence	A sentence expresses a *complete* thought. A sentence *begins with a capital letter* and *ends with a period*.
Capital Letter	*Uppercase letter* as underlined below. <u>A</u> a
Subject	The person, place or thing that *is being talked about* in a sentence.
Predicate	The part of the sentence *containing the verb and telling you what the subject is doing*.

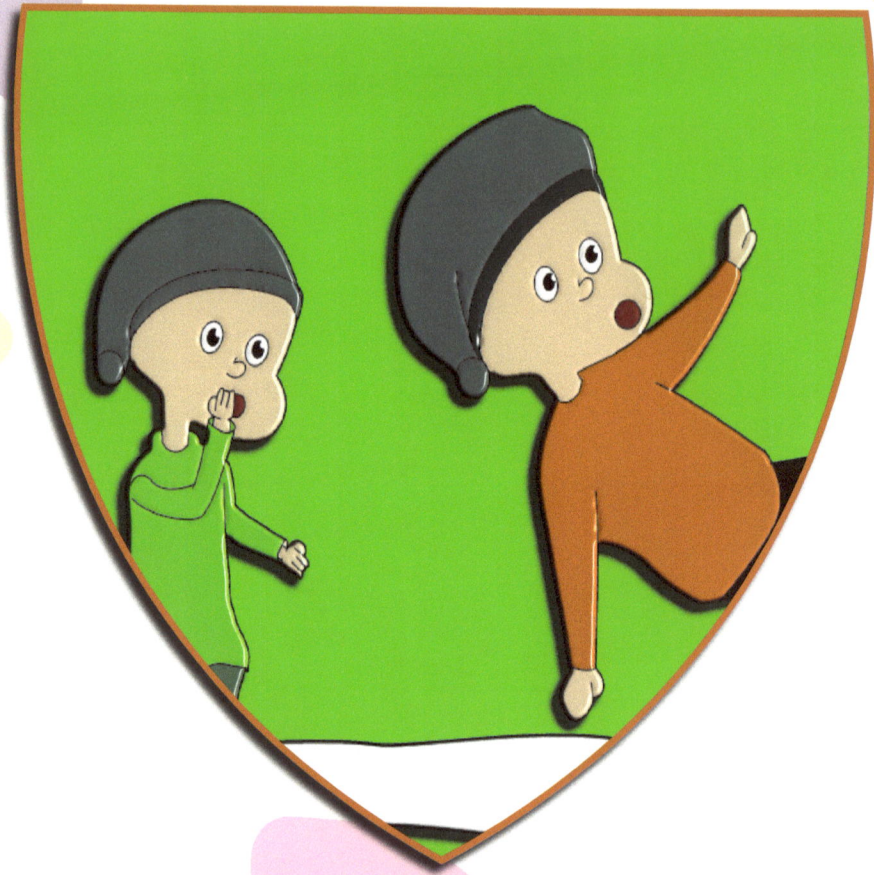

GUIDE # 2

BUILDING-BLOCKS OF READING

PUNCTUATION MARKS AND THEIR MEANINGS

Period	Tells you when a sentence has ended.
Comma	Signals a break in a sentence, but does not end a sentence. Example: One day, I was riding in the car with my dad.
Question Mark	Follows a sentence that requests information. Example: Why do people want buy gross things?
Exclamation Point	Used to indicate someone is expressing emotion. Example: Ouch!
Quotation Marks	Tells you someone is actually speaking. Example: Bob said: "What do you mean son?"
Semicolon	Functions in the same manner as and. Example: We are going out; we'll be back tomorrow.
Apostrophe	Used to indicate that a thing belongs to someone or something. Example: Avien used dad's computer to find the answer.

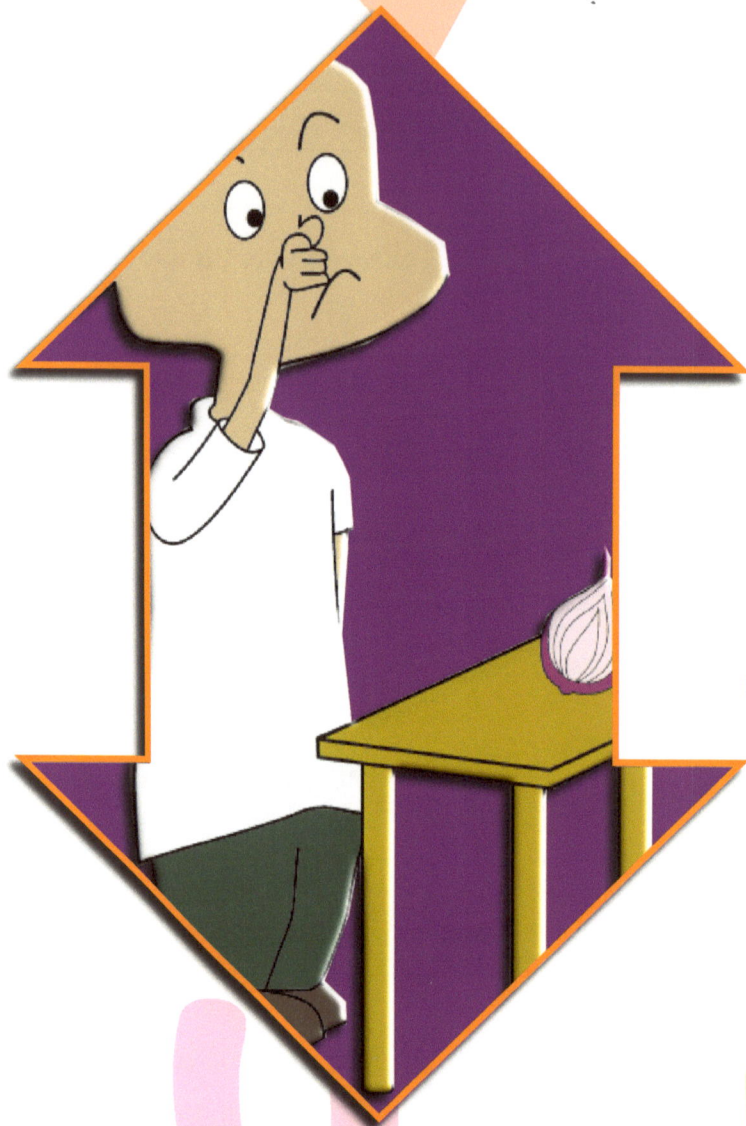

GUIDE # 3

BUILDING-BLOCKS OF READING

THE FOUR BASIC SENTENCE TYPES AND THEIR FUNCTIONS

DECLARATIVE SENTENCE

Function: Makes a statement.

I like cheese.

INTERROGATIVE SENTENCE

Function: Asks a question.

Why do you like cheese?

EXCLAMATORY SENTENCE

Function: Expresses emotion.

Cheese is delicious!

IMPERATIVE SENTENCE

Function: Gives a command.

Don't touch my cheese.

GUIDE # 4

THE BASIC PARTS OF A PARAGRAPH

OPENING SENTENCE

Function: Tells the topic or main idea of the paragraph.

DETAILS

Function: Explains or proves the topic sentence.

CLOSING SENTENCE

Function: Adds a final comment or idea from the writer.

NOTE

A paragraph is like a hamburger. The opening and closing sentences are the pieces of the bun on the top and bottom. The details are the meat and cheese in the middle of the hamburger.

There are many benefits that reading passes on to those who make reading a daily practice. Although reading provides many benefits, there are four that we think are the most important.

First, reading keeps you safe. Second, reading increases your vocabulary, third, reading makes you a better reader and most importantly, reading increases your knowledge about the world.

If you would like improve your ability to do these things, you should read everyday. You should do this even if you do not like to read. You'll be happy that you did.

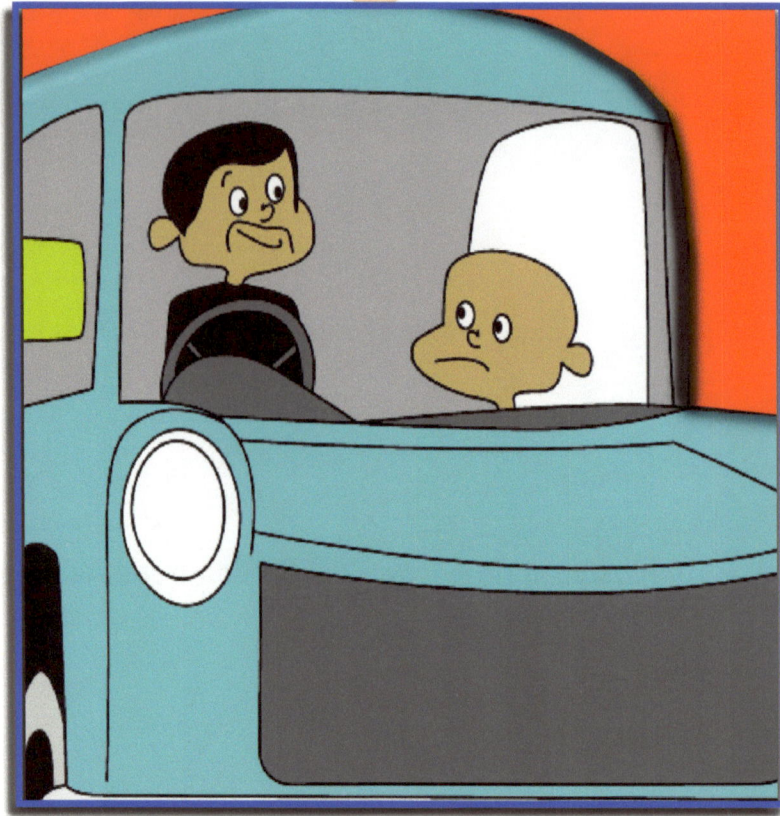

CHALLENGE # 1

DO YOU KNOW YOUR PUNCTUATION?

1.) Write a PERIOD in the red box.

2.) Write a QUESTION MARK in the red box.

3.) Write an EXCLAMATION MARK in the red box.

4.) Write a QUOTATION MARK in the red box.

5.) Write a COMMA in the red box.

6.) Write a SEMI-COLON in the red box.

7.) Write a DASH in the red box.

8,) Write an APOSTROPHE in the red box.

CHALLENGE # 2

DRAW A LINE FROM PUNCTUATION TO FUNCTION

BEGINS A SENTENCE

?

!

EXPRESSES A COMPLETE THOUGHT

ENDS A SENTENCE

CAPITAL LETTER

GATHERS INFORMATION

SENTENCE

EXPRESSES EMOTION

CHALLENGE # 3

TEST YOUR KNOWLEDGE

1.) Who is the main character of the story?

2.) Name two things that the main character learned.

3.) What is the most important thing that the main character learned by the end of the story?

4.) Can you give the meaning of three new words that you learned in this story?

5.) What is the overall message of the story?

CHALLENGE # 4

= 1 PT

COMPLETE THE SENTENCES BELOW USING THESE WORDS.

End	Expands	Beginning	Daily
	Question	Thing	Make Sense

1. Reading helps you _____ of your Random Thoughts.

2. Reading should be a _____ practice.

3. Reading is important because it _____ your mind.

4. A capital letter comes at the _____ of a sentence.

5. A period comes at the _____ of a sentence.

6. An Interrogative sentence asks a _____.

7. A Noun is a person, place or _____.

CHALLENGE # 5

TEST YOUR KNOWLEDGE

1. One of the marks below shows a question has been asked, which one is it?

?   .   !   66   ;   :

2. These marks shows someone is speaking. Which mark is it?

?   .   !   66   ;   :

3. This mark ends a statement. Which mark is it?

?   .   !   66   ;   :

4. This mark expresses emotion. Which mark is it?

?   .   !   66   ;   :

5. This mark shows a close relationship between two sentences . Which mark is it?

?   .   !   66   ;   :

CHALLENGE # 6

CIRCLE ALL OF THE ADJECTIVES IN THE CHART BELOW

Cold	White	Gross	Man
Slippery	Shoe	Tree	Run
Read	House	Cat	Car
Computer	Desk	Grocery	Book
Frosty	Family	Onion	Fluffy
Careful	Painful	Table	Cool
Parent	Teacher	Period	Warm
Random	Clothes	Different	Question
Ground	Red	Dangerous	Thoughts
Sidewalk	Brother	Small	Sled
Winter	Learn	New	Word
Thing	Water	Rain	Blue
Big	Fast	Black	Woman
Sister	Yellow	Book	Good
Hot	Purple	Best	Happy
Green	Ten	Sad	Orange
Ride	Light	Chuckle	Dad
Home	Hat	Glove	Word

CHALLENGE # 7

Underline All Of The Nouns In The Chart Below

= 1 PT

Cold	White	Gross	Man
Slippery	Shoe	Tree	Run
Read	House	Cat	Car
Computer	Desk	Grocery	Book
Frosty	Family	Onion	Fluffy
Careful	Painful	Table	Cool
Parent	Teacher	Period	Warm
Random	Clothes	Different	Question
Ground	Red	Dangerous	Thoughts
Sidewalk	Brother	Small	Sled
Winter	Learn	New	Word
Thing	Water	Rain	Blue
Big	Fast	Black	Woman
Sister	Yellow	Book	Good
Hot	Purple	Best	Happy
Green	Ten	Sad	Orange
Ride	Light	Chuckle	Dad
Home	Hat	Glove	Word

CHALLENGE # 8

PARAGRAPH WRITING

= 1 PT

WRITE A PARAGRAPH USING THE GUIDE ON PAGE 28.

= .5 PT

= .5 PT